CAVIARE AT
THE FUNERAL

CAVIARE AT THE FUNERAL

poems by

LOUIS SIMPSON

FRANKLIN WATTS
New York / Toronto
1980

The author acknowledges permission from the fol-
lowing publishers to reprint poems: The Gallery
Press, The Deerfield Press, The Pomegranate Press,
*The Listener, Newsday, The Paris Review, The
Iowa Review, The Missouri Review, The Ohio Re-
view, Critical Quarterly, The American Poetry
Review, New Statesman, Forum, Poetry East, Pauma-
nok Rising, Harvard Magazine, Harpoon.*

"Working Late" and "The Pawnshop" originally
appeared in *The New Yorker.*

"A River Running By" and "Back in the States"
are reprinted by permission of *The Georgia Review.*

"As a Man Walks," "A Nuclear Family," "A Bush
Band," and "Death of Thunderbolt" originally ap-
peared in *Armidale* (Poems and a Prose Memoir by
Louis Simpson), BOA Pamphlet Series A, No. 5,
BOA Editions, 92 Park Avenue, Brockport, N.Y.
14420. Copyright © 1979 by Louis Simpson.

"Unfinished Life," "Typhus," "The Art of Story-
telling," and "Caviare at the Funeral" are re-
printed by permission of *The American Poetry
Review.*

Library of Congress Cataloging in Publication Data

Simpson, Louis Aston Marantz, 1923–
Caviare at the funeral.

I. Title.
PS3537.I75C3   811'.54   80–16217
ISBN 0-531-09937-7
ISBN (Paperback Edition) 0-531-09951-2

OTHER BOOKS
BY LOUIS SIMPSON

Poetry

The Arrivistes: Poems 1940–1949

*Good News of Death
and Other Poems*

A Dream of Governors

At the End of the Open Road

Selected Poems

Adventures of the Letter I

Searching for the Ox

Prose

James Hogg: A Critical Study

Riverside Drive

An Introduction to Poetry

North of Jamaica

*Three on the Tower:
The Lives and Works of
Ezra Pound, T. S. Eliot
and William Carlos Williams*

*A Revolution in Taste:
Studies of Dylan Thomas,
Allen Ginsberg, Sylvia Plath
and Robert Lowell*

CONTENTS

I

II

III

IV

*Restlessness is a sign of intelligence;
revulsion, the flight of a soul.*

CAVIARE AT
THE FUNERAL

I

WORKING LATE

A light is on in my father's study.
"Still up?" he says, and we are silent,
looking at the harbor lights,
listening to the surf
and the creak of coconut boughs.

He is working late on cases.
No impassioned speech! He argues from evidence,
actually pacing out and measuring,
while the fans revolving on the ceiling
winnow the true from the false.

Once he passed a brass curtain rod
through a head made out of plaster
and showed the jury the angle of fire—
where the murderer must have stood.
For years, all through my childhood,
if I opened a closet . . . bang!
There would be the dead man's head
with a black hole in the forehead.

All the arguing in the world
will not stay the moon.
She has come all the way from Russia
to gaze for a while in a mango tree
and light the wall of a veranda,
before resuming her interrupted journey
beyond the harbor and the lighthouse
at Port Royal, turning away
from land to the open sea.

Yet, nothing in nature changes, from that
        day to this,
she is still the mother of us all.
I can see the drifting offshore lights,
black posts where the pelicans brood.

And the light that used to shine
at night in my father's study
now shines as late in mine.

NEW LOTS

On the Sabbath when darkness falls
Pearl Wanateck feeds her hungry ghosts.
Standing before the candles
she prays . . . for all the world
and her relatives over in Russia.

I have seen them in photographs . . .
One pale rabbinical face . . .
wearing an overcoat that is too long
and yet too short in the sleeves,
standing with his back to a wall.

In the next he has got himself married.
There are two children, a boy and a girl.
This was some time ago. The village
and all who dwelled therein
have been swept from the face of the earth.

II

The candles cast shadows on the wall.
Hungry ghosts! Not one stalwart tiller of the soil
among them . . . Their unreal occupations!
One works for a theatrical agency,
one at Charles of the Ritz,
one for a stockbrokers' firm.

As though when they left the Old Country
and the streets knee-deep in mud
they swore an oath: Never again!
It would be nothing but steam heat from now on
and carpeting, wall to wall.
They would take ship to the highest city
and cling there, looking down.

Creeping out at twilight to a restaurant
and a show, then back again.

High above the lighted city
the traffic is hushed.
There are only voices coming from a radio.

It is time now for Jack Benny.

III

Gefilte fish . . .
carrots and radishes, chicken soup,
boiled chicken and boiled beef . . .
Please pass the horseradish.

Beth is talking . . . about her work at the Ritz.
Yesterday they had a crisis—
Miss Martin's hairdresser called in sick.
She didn't kick up a fuss—
Miss Martin isn't like other celebrities,
though she is a star she's a lady.

Now Dave . . . He works in Whelan's drugstore
on Broadway. They get all sorts of people . . .
actors who are "at liberty,"
shoplifters, people looking for an argument.

He noticed a customer taking lipstick
from the display case and testing it on her arm.
When he went across and spoke to her
"You can kiss my foot!" she cried.
She went hurriedly out . . .
At the door she turned and stuck out her tongue.

He finishes. No one says anything
until, finally, Grandmother speaks:
"There are a lot of miserable people."

"Yes," someone remarks, "especially in New York."

18]

IV

Making the return journey by subway . . .
At Forty-Second Street I get off and walk.
I like to look in the windows
at fountain pens and knives,
back-date magazines . . .
the liner in the window of the travel agency
waving good-bye . . .

But what about the others
who stay?

"A farm was growing in the midst of Paris
and its windows looked out on the Milky Way."
So it is with Dave. After so many years
waiting on customers . . . and his feet hurt . . .
he still thinks it worth it, to have seen
so many famous celebrities, stars of stage and screen.

He once had a conversation with Jolson:
"I have a chiropodist who's a whiz,"
Al told him, and wrote down the address.
"When you're in L.A. look him up,
just tell him Al sent you."

People like the woman in the drugstore . . .
I keep seeing her in a room
in one of the cheap residential hotels
close to Times Square and the theater . . .
seated next to a radiator
in a bathrobe, drying her hair.
Sections of newspaper strewn on the floor . . .

Listening to her breathe . . .
A faucet drips, the radiator hisses,
there is a siren off somewhere.

SWAY

"Swing and sway with Sammy Kaye"

Everyone at Lake Kearney had a nickname:
there was a Bumstead, a Tonto, a Tex,
and, from the slogan of a popular orchestra,
two sisters, Swing and Sway.

Swing jitterbugged, hopping around
on the dance floor, working up a sweat.
Sway was beautiful. My heart went out to her
when she lifted her heavy rack of dishes
and passed through the swinging door.

She was engaged, to an enlisted man
who was stationed at Fort Dix.
He came once or twice on weekends
to see her. I tried talking to him,
but he didn't answer . . . out of stupidity
or dislike, I could not tell which.
In real life he was a furniture salesman.
This was the hero on whom she had chosen
to bestow her affections.

I told her of my ambition:
to write novels conveying the excitement
of life . . . the main building lit up
like a liner on Saturday night;
the sound of the band . . . clarinet,
saxophone, snare drum, piano.
He who would know your heart (America)
must seek it in your songs.

And the contents of your purse . . .
among Kleenex, aspirin,
chewing gum wrappers, combs, et cetera.

"Don't stop," she said, "I'm listening.
Here it is!" flourishing her lighter.

In the afternoon when the dishes were washed
and tables wiped, we rowed out on the lake.
I read aloud . . . *The Duino Elegies,*
while she reclined, one shapely knee up,
trailing a hand in the water.

She had chestnut-colored hair.
Her eyes were changing like the surface
with ripples and the shadows of clouds.

"Beauty," I read to her, "is nothing
but beginning of Terror we're still just able to bear."

She came from Jersey, the industrial wasteland
behind which Manhattan suddenly rises.
I could visualize the street where she lived,
and see her muffled against the cold,
in galoshes, trudging to school.
Running about in tennis shoes
all through the summer . . .
I could hear the porch swing squeak
and see into the parlor.
It was divided by a curtain or screen . . .

"That's it," she said, "all but the screen.
There isn't any."

When she or her sister had a boyfriend
their mother used to stay in the parlor,
pretending to sew, and keeping an eye on them
like Fate.

At night she would lie awake
looking at the sky, spangled over.
Her thoughts were as deep and wide as the sky.
As time went by she had a feeling
of missing out . . . that everything
was happening somewhere else.

Some of the kids she grew up with
went crazy . . . like a car turning over and over.
One of her friends had been beaten
by the police. Some vital fluid
seemed to have gone out of him.
His arms and legs shook. Busted springs.

———

She said, "When you're a famous novelist
will you write about me?"

I promised . . . and tried to keep my promise.

Recently, looking for a toolbox,
I came upon some typewritten pages,
all about her. There she is
in a canoe . . . a gust of wind
rustling the leaves along the shore.
Playing tennis, running up and down the baseline.
Down by the boathouse, listening to the orchestra
playing "Sleepy Lagoon."

Then the trouble begins. I can never think of anything
to make the characters do.
We are still sitting in the moonlight
while she finishes her cigarette.
Two people go by, talking in low voices.
A car door slams. Driving off . . .

"I suppose we ought to go,"
I say.
                    And she says, "Not yet."

BASIC BLUES

Three comrades . . . there are always three.
The one with his cap cocked rakishly
tosses a coin, and they're off.

But it's hopeless. Ever since Pearl Harbor
all the women have been hidden away
as though by magic. The length of Main Street,
and Market, and Figueroa . . .

                              They keep walking
past houses with lawns and trees.
In an area where there are benches
they sit and gaze at the grass being watered
and the names of flowers and trees:
Pyracantha, Golden Rain Tree,
Ceniza.

A vagrant breeze rustles the leaves
and they become aware that time is passing.
They take the bus back to town.
By now it is the middle of the afternoon,
the light on concrete is glittering,
the heat rising in waves.
They hold another sidewalk conferencce
and decide to settle for the movie.

————

It's time to return to the depot
and the ride back . . .
                         looking at fields,
small trees,
houses like wooden boxes,
a church that says "Praise the Lord."

————

They've been traveling for hours.
When the bus brakes for a stop
the sleepers stir
and someone asks, "What time is it?"

The streets are dark and desolate.
O, all the wars in Germany
and Russia will not make them grieve
like a Shell station, and Lone Star Bar,
and the Hotel Davy Crockett.

ON THE LEDGE

I can see the coast coming near . . .
one of our planes, a Thunderbolt, plunging down
and up again. Seconds later
we heard the rattle of machine guns.

That night we lay among hedgerows.
The night was black. There was thrashing
in a hedgerow, a burst of firing . . .
in the morning, a dead cow.

A plane droned overhead . . .
one of theirs,
diesel, with a rhythmic sound.
Then the bombs came whistling down.

———

We were strung out on an embankment
side by side in a straight line,
like infantry in World War One
waiting for the whistle to blow.

The Germans knew we were there
and were firing everything they had,
bullets passing right above.
I knew that in a moment the order would come.

There is a page in Dostoevsky
about a man being given the choice
to die, or to stand on a ledge
through all eternity . . .

alive and breathing the air,
looking at the trees, and sky . . .
the wings of a butterfly
as it drifts from stem to stem.

But men who have stepped off the ledge
know all that there is to know:
who survived the Bloody Angle,
Verdun, the first day on the Somme.

As it turned out, we didn't have to.
Instead, they used Typhoons.
They flew over our heads, firing rockets
on the German positions.

So it was easy. We just strolled
over the embankment,
and down the other side,
and across an open field.

Yet, like the man on the ledge,
I still haven't moved . . .
watching an ant
climb a blade of grass and climb back down.

A BOWER OF ROSES

The mixture of smells—
of Algerian tobacco,
wine barrels, and urine—
I'll never forget it,
he thought, if I live to be a hundred.

And the whores in every street,
and like flies in the bars . . .
Some of them looked familiar:
there was a Simone Simone,
a Veronica.

And some were original,
like the two who stood on a corner,
a brunette with hair like ink
and a platinum blonde,
holding a Great Dane on a leash.

"A monster," said Margot.
"Those two give me the shivers."

The other girls were of the same opinion.
One said, "And, after all,
think what a dog like that must cost to feed."

This was conclusive. They stared out at the street—
there was nothing more to be said.

———

When they gave him a pass at the hospital
he would make for the bar in Rue Sainte Apolline
Margot frequented. Sitting in a corner
as though she had been waiting . . .

27]

Like the sweetheart on a postcard
gazing from a bower of roses . . .
"Je t'attends toujours."

For ten thousand francs
she would let him stay the night,
and a thousand for the concièrge.
The maid, too, must have something.

Then, finally, he would be alone with her.
Her face a perfect oval,
a slender neck, brown hair . . .

It surprised him that a girl
who looked delicate in her clothes
was voluptuous when she stood naked.

———

He caught up with the division in Germany,
at Dusseldorf, living in houses
a hundred yards from the Rhine.

Now and then a shell flew over.
For every shell Krupp fired
General Motors sent back four.

Division found some cases of beer,
and cigars, and passed them around—
a taste of the luxury
that was coming. The post-war.

One morning they crossed the Rhine.
Then they were marching through villages
where the people stood and stared.
Then they rode in convoys of trucks
on the autobahns. Deeper in.

The areas on the map of Germany
marked with the swastika kept diminishing,
and then, one day, there were none left.

———

They were ordered back to France,
only sixty kilometers from Paris.

Once more he found himself climbing the stairs.
He knocked, and heard footsteps.
"Who is it?"
                        The door opened a crack,
then wide, and he was holding her.
"My God," she said, "chéri,
I never thought to see you again."

That night, lying next to her,
he thought about young women
he had known back in the States
who would not let you do anything.
And a song of the first war . . .
"How Are You Going to Keep Them Down on the Farm?
(After They've Seen Paree)."

He supposed this was what life taught you,
that words you thought were a joke,
and applied to someone else,
were real, and applied to you.

II

AMERICAN CLASSIC

It's a classic American scene—
a car stopped off the road
and a man trying to repair it.

The woman who stays in the car
in the classic American scene
stares back at the freeway traffic.

They look surprised, and ashamed
to be so helpless . . .
let down in the middle of the road!

To think that their car would do this!
They look like mountain people
whose son has gone against the law.

But every night they set out food
and the robber goes skulking back to the trees.
That's how it is with the car . . .

it's theirs, they're stuck with it.
Now they know what it's like to sit
and see the world go whizzing by.

In the fume of carbon monoxide and dust
they are not such good Americans
as they thought they were.

The feeling of being left out
through no fault of your own, is common.
That's why I say, an American classic.

LITTLE COLORED FLAGS

Lines of little colored flags
advertising Foreign Motor Sales . . .
Mario's, the beauty salon,
the hardware store with its display
of wheelbarrows and garbage cans . . .

Most people here are content
to make a decent living.
They take pride in their homes and raising a family.
The women attend meetings of the P.T.A.
Sometimes they drive in to New York
for a day's shopping and the theater.
Their husbands belong to the golf club
or the yacht club.
It makes sense to own a boat if you live in the area.

They go on vacation to Bermuda,
or Europe. Even the Far East.

There aren't too many alternatives.
The couple sitting in the car
will either decide to go home
or to a motel.
Afterwards, they may continue
to see each other, in which case
there will probably be a divorce,
or else they may decide
to stop seeing each other.

Another favorite occupation is gardening . . .
wind rushing in the leaves like a sea.
And the sea itself is there
behind the last house at the end of the street.

THE BEADED PEAR

Kennst du das Land, wo die Zitronen blüh'n?
                    Goethe, "Mignon"

1 *Shopping*

Dad in Bermuda shorts, Mom her hair in curlers,
Jimmy, sixteen, and Darlene who is twelve,
are walking through the Smith Haven Mall.

Jimmy needs a new pair of shoes.
In the Mall by actual count
there are twenty-two stores selling shoes:
Wise Shoes, Regal Shoes,
National Shoes, Naturalizer Shoes,
Stride Rite, Selby, Hanover . . .

Dad has to buy a new lock for the garage,
Mom and Darlene want to look at clothes.
They agree to meet again in an hour
at the fountain.

The Mall is laid out like a cathedral
with two arcades that cross—
Macy's at one end of the main arcade,
Abraham and Straus at the other.
At the junction of transept and nave
there is a circular, sunken area
with stairs where people sit,
mostly teenagers, smoking
and making dates to meet later.
This is what is meant by "at the fountain."

2 *"Why don't you get transferred, Dad?"*

One of Jimmy's friends comes by in his car,
and Jimmy goes out. "Be careful,"
Mom says. He has to learn to drive,
but it makes her nervous thinking about it.

Darlene goes over to see Marion
whose father is being transferred
to a new branch of the company
in Houston. "Why don't you get transferred, Dad?"

"I'd like to," he replies.
"I'd also like a million dollars."

This is a constant topic in the family:
where else you would like to live.
Darlene likes California—
"It has beautiful scenery
and you get to meet all the stars."
Mom prefers Arizona, because of a picture
she saw once, in *Good Housekeeping*.
Jimmy doesn't care,
and Dad likes it here. "You can find anything
you want right where you are."
He reminds them of *The Wizard of Oz,*
about happiness, how it is found
right in your own backyard.

Dad's right, Mom always says.
The Wizard of Oz is a tradition
in the family. They see it every year.

3 The Beaded Pear

The children are home at six,
and they sit down to eat. Mom insists
on their eating together at least once
every week. It keeps the family together.

After helping with the dishes
the children go out again,
and Mom and Dad settle down to watch
"Hollywood Star Time," with Bobby Darin,
Buddy Rich, Laura Nyro,
Judy Collins, and Stevie Wonder.

When this is over he looks in *TV Guide,*
trying to decide
whether to watch "Salty O'Rourke (1945).
A gambler who is readying his horse
for an important race
falls in love with a pretty teacher,"
or, "Delightful family fare,
excellent melodrama of the Mafia."

She has seen enough television
for one night. She gets out the beaded pear
she bought today in the Mall.

A "Special $1.88 do-it-yourself Beaded Pear.
No glueing or sewing required.
Beautiful beaded fruit is easily assembled
using enclosed pins, beads, and decorative material."

She says, "It's not going to be so easy."

"No," he says, "it never is."

She speaks again. "There is a complete series.
Apple, Pear, Banana, Lemon, Orange,
Grapes, Strawberry, Plum, and Lime."

THE ICE CUBE MAKER

Once the ice was in a tray.
You would hold it under a faucet
till the cubes came unstuck, in a block.
Then you had to run more water over it
until, finally, the cubes came loose.

Later on, there was a handle you lifted,
breaking out the ice cubes.
But still it was a nuisance—
in order to get at one ice cube
you had to melt the whole tray.

Then they invented the ice cube maker
which makes cubes individually,
letting them fall in a container
until it is full, when it stops.
You can just reach in and take ice cubes.

———

When her husband came home he saw that she was drunk.
He changed into an old shirt and slacks.
He stared at the screen door in the kitchen . . .
the screen had to be replaced.
He wondered what he was doing. Why fix it?

MAGRITTE SHAVING

How calm the torso of a woman,
like a naked statue . . .
her right leg painted blue,
her left leg colored saffron.
In an alcove . . . The window yields
a view of earth, yellow fields.

―――――

Objects that you may hold loom large:
a wine-glass, a shaving brush.
The furniture in the room is small:
a bed, a closet with mirrors . . .
in the room without walls
in the sky full of clouds.

―――――

The sphere, colored orange, floating in space
has a face with fixed brown eyes.
Below the sphere, a shirt with a tie
in a dark, formal suit
stands facing you, close to the parapet
on the edge of the canyon.

A RIVER RUNNING BY

The air was aglimmer, thousands of snowflakes
falling the length of the street.

Five to eight inches, said the radio.
But in the car it was warm;
she had left the engine running
and sat with both hands on the wheel,
her breast and throat like marble
rising from the pool of the dark.

She apologized for the mess:
the litter of junk mail,
an old pair of sneakers,
a suspicious-looking brown paper bag,
and a tennis racket. She had been meaning
to get rid of it. All last summer
she had wondered why her arm hurt,
until a few days ago when she noticed
that the frame was bent.
                              She played tennis
the way she did everything, carelessly.
She hadn't deserved to win,
one woman told her, lacking the right attitude.

———

The fallen snow gleamed in the dark
like water. Everything is a flowing,
you have only to flow with it.

If you did, you would live to regret it.
After a while, passion would wear off
and you would still be faced with life,
the same old dull routine.

They would quarrel and make up
regularly. Within a few years
he would grow morose. The trouble with love
is that you have to believe in it.
Like swimming . . . you have to keep it up.

And those who didn't, who remained
on the sofa watching television,
would live to wish that they had.
It was six of one and half a dozen of the other.

"You're serious. What are you thinking?"

That the snow looks like a river.
But there is no river, it is only an idea,
he thought, standing on the edge.

41]

AN AFFAIR
IN THE COUNTRY

As he lived on East 82nd Street
and she in Wappingers Falls
he saw more of the road than of her:

Kaufman Carpet
Outlook Realty
Scelfo Realty   Amoco   Color TV

Now and then there would be something out of the ordinary:
X-Rated Dancer
Fabric Gardens   Discount Dog Food

They would meet for a couple of hours
at the Holiday Inn. Then she would have to leave,
and he had to start back.

Speed Zone Ahead
Signal Ahead
Road Narrows
Bridge Out
Yield

THE OLD GRAVEYARD
AT HAUPPAUGE

In Adam's fall we sinned all,
and fell out of Paradise
into mankind—this body of salt
and gathering of the waters,
birth, work, and wedding garment.

But now we are at rest . . .
Aletta and Phebe Almira,
and Augusta Bunce, and the MacCrones . . .
lying in the earth, looking up
at the clouds and drifting trees.

UNFINISHED LIFE

The "villages" begin further out . . .
post office, high school, bank,
built of brick. The state of mind
is Colonial: four white columns
and a watchtower, also white.

Then screens of trees and evergreens
hide the houses, mile on mile.
When the traffic slows to a halt
your eye is attracted to fragments:
a tailpipe, rusted through,
a hubcap, two feet of chain.
Like a battlefield, some great clash of armor . . .

A slice of black rubber
that has crawled out of a crack
and lies on the road like a snake . . .

Not to mention the guardrail
wrenched and twisted out of shape.

You can visualize the accident:
blood seeping in white hair,
turning it cherry-red.

———

She said, "I'll be in the garden
if there is anything you need."

He thanked her, and she left,
closing the door silently.
He opened the box and began to read.
Two hours later he was still at it:

"I am sitting with Van Meer,
the old church to our left,
a new 'American' drugstore across the street—
'drugstore publicis' it says repeatedly.
And the Cinema Saint Germain,
showing 'Les Galets d'Etretats' . . .
a woman named Virna Lisi with her mouth open.
A sign saying "Henressy," and the time
in changing numbers.
A 'Brasserie Lipp.'
A pole, painted white, from which a tricolor hangs.
Rue Bonaparte angling left,
making a flatiron with Rue Rennes.
More signs—'Ted Lapidus,' 'Disques Raoul Vidal.' "

The obsession with names and signs,
Peter thought, could be a sign of senility.
Nevertheless, the writing was good,
especially in the places the public would want to read:
his early days in the Village,
then with Norton-Harjes overseas,
and Paris after the war.

The manuscript came to a stop
with a screech of tires, a crash.

A hubcap went rolling in circles,
ringing as it settled.

———

J. B. tapped with a pencil
on the box . . . swung in his chair
and gazed out the window
at the helmeted head of Minerva
in bas-relief on the adjacent building
where none but a head editor
could see it, and the pigeons.
Sub specie aeternitatis.

Swung back again . . . "We'll take it,
but you'll have to write a conclusion.
Why do you look," he said, "so dismayed?
You did an outstanding job with *Monica*."

This was a historical romance.
The author, a Southern lady, went insane,
and Peter wrote the missing chapters.

"Couldn't we just end with a note
saying that he left it unfinished?"

"No" said J. B., "I don't think so."
He had the look on his face—inspiration.
There was no arguing with it—
the look he had when he signed the contract
for the cookbook that sold a million.

It was also the look that had turned down
Cards of Identity and *Go Tell It on the Mountain.*

He handed the manuscript over . . .
"It needs some final view of things."

———

Profession of Faith

As a writer I imagine characters,
giving them definite features
and bodies, a color of hair.
I imagine what they feel
and, finally, make them speak.

Increasingly I have come to believe
that the things we imagine
are not amusements, they are real.

There stands my wife, in the garden
gathering lilacs . . . reaching up,
pulling a branch toward her,
severing the flower with a knife
decisively, like a surgeon.

If I go away, into another country,
all that will remain is a memory.

Once, on a cold winter's night,
driving on a winding road,
fields covered with snow on my left,
on my right a dark body of water,
I conjured up the figure of a man
standing or floating in mid-air.

The things we see and the things we imagine,
afterwards, when you think about them,
are equally composed of words.

It is the words we use, finally,
that matter, if anything does.

———

The last time I saw Van Meer,
if the reader recalls, we were at the Deux Magots
looking across the street
at a *brasserie* and a drugstore,
with people strolling past:
a man with a moustache, wearing a homburg,
the *Légion d'honneur*
in his buttonhole. His wife
in gray, equally distinguished.
Two students, a boy and girl
with dark, nervous eyes.
An old woman, her feet wrapped in rags,
one of the *clochards*
who sleep beneath the bridges.
And the tourists. This year
there is a swarm of Japanese . . .
staring at the people in the café,
the people in the café staring back.
Life, that feeds on the spectacle of itself
to no purpose . . .

He said, "We are, you and I,
in eternity. The difference between us
and them is that we know it."

Shortly after this he died.
But everything is still there.

The shadow of the word
flitting over the scene,
the street and motionless crowd.

III

WHY DO YOU WRITE
ABOUT RUSSIA?

When I was a child
my mother told stories about the country
she came from. Wolves were howling,
snow fell, the drunken Cossack
shouted in the snow.

Rats prowled the floor of the cellar
where the children slept.
Once, after an illness, she was sent
to Odessa, on the sea. There were battleships
painted white, and ladies and gentlemen
walking the esplanade . . . white naval uniforms
and parasols.

These stories were told
against a background of tropical night . . .
a sea breeze stirring the flowers
that open at dusk, smelling like perfume.
The voice that spoke of freezing cold
itself was warm and infinitely comforting.

So it is with poetry: whatever numbing horrors
it may speak of, the voice itself
tells of love and infinite wonder.

Later, when I came to New York,
I used to go to my grandmother's
in Brooklyn. The names of stations
return in their order like a charm:
Franklin, Nostrand, Kingston.

And members of the family gather:
the three sisters, the one brother,
one of the cousins from Washington,
and myself . . . a "student at Columbia."
But what am I really?

For when my grandmother says, "Eat!
People who work with their heads have to eat more" . . .
Work? Does it deserve a name
so full of seriousness and high purpose?
Gazing across Amsterdam Avenue
at the windows opposite, letting my mind
wander where it will, from the page
to Malaya, or some street in Paris . . .
Drifting smoke. The end will be as fatal
as an opium-eater's dream.

———

The view has changed—to evergreens,
a hedge, and my neighbor's roof.
This too is like a dream, the way we live
with our cars and power-mowers . . .
a life that shuns emotion
and the violence that goes with it,
the object being to live quietly
and bring up children to be happy.

Yes, but what are you going to tell them
of what lies ahead?
That the better life seems
the more it goes sour? The child no longer
a child, his happiness all of a sudden
behind him. And he in turn
expected to bring up his children
to be happy . . .

What then do I want?

A life in which there are depths
beyond happiness. As one of my friends,
Grigoryev, says, "Two things
constantly cry out in creation,
the sea and man's soul."

Reaching from where we are
to where we came from . . . *Thalassa!*
a view of the sea.

———

I sit listening to the rasp
of a power-saw, the puttering of a motorboat.
The whole meaningless life around me
affirming a positive attitude . . .

When a hat appears, a black felt hat,
gliding along the hedge . . .
then a long, black overcoat
that falls beneath the knee.

He produces a big, purple handkerchief,
brushes off a chair, and sits.

"It's hot," he says, "but I like to walk,
that way you get to see the world.
And so, what are you reading now?"

Chekhov, I tell him.

"Of course. But have you read Leskov?
There are sentences that will stay in your mind
a whole lifetime.
For instance, in the 'Lady Macbeth,'
when the woman says to her lover,
'You couldn't be nearly as desirous
as you say you are, for I heard you singing' . . .
he answers, 'What about gnats?
They sing all their lives, but it's not for joy.' "

So my imaginary friend tells stories
of the same far place the soul comes from.

When I think about Russia
it's not that area of the earth's surface
with Leningrad to the West and Siberia
to the East—I don't know anything
about the continental mass.

It's a sound, such as you hear
in a sea breaking along a shore.

My people came from Russia,
bringing with them nothing
but that sound.

TYPHUS

"The whole earth was covered with snow,
and the Snow Queen's sleigh came gliding.
I heard the bells behind me,
and ran, and ran, till I was out of breath."

During the typhus epidemic
she almost died, and would have
but for the woman who lived next door
who cooked for her and watched by the bed.

When she came back to life
and saw herself in a mirror
they had cut off all her hair.
Also, they had burned her clothing,
and her doll, the only one she ever had,
made out of rags and a stick.

Afterwards, they sent her away
to Odessa, to stay with relatives.
The day she was leaving for home
she bought some plums, as a gift
to take back to the family.
They had never seen such plums!
They were in a window, in a basket.
To buy them she spent her last few kopecks.

The journey took three days by train.
It was hot, and the plums were beginning to spoil.
So she ate them . . .
until, finally, all were gone.
The people on the train were astonished.
A child who would eat a plum
and cry . . . then eat another!

———

Her sister, Lisa, died of typhus.
The corpse was laid on the floor.

They carried it to the cemetery
in a box, and brought back the box.
"We were poor—a box was worth something."

THE ART OF
STORYTELLING

Once upon a time there was a *shocket,*
that is, a kosher butcher,
who went for a walk.

He was standing by the harbor
admiring the ships, all painted white,
when up came three sailors, led by an officer.
"Filth," they said, "who gave you permission?"
and they seized and carried him off.

So he was taken into the navy.
It wasn't a bad life—nothing is.
He learned how to climb and sew,
and to shout "Glad to be of service, Your Excellency!"
He sailed all round the world,
was twice shipwrecked, and had other adventures.
Finally, he made his way back to the village . . .
whereupon he put on his apron, and picked up his knife,
and continued to be a shocket.

At this point, the person telling the story
would say, "This shocket-sailor
was one of our relatives, a distant cousin."

It was always so, they knew they could depend on it.
Even if the story made no sense,
the one in the story would be a relative—
a definite connection with the family.

THE PAWNSHOP

The first time I saw a pawnshop
I thought, Sheer insanity.
A revolver lying next to a camera,
violins hanging in the air like hams . . .

But in fact there was a reason for everything.

So it is with all these lives:
one is stained from painting with oils;
another has a way of arguing
with a finger along his nose, the Misnagid tradition;
a third sits at a desk made of mahogany.

They are all cunningly displayed
to appeal to someone. Each has its place in the universe.

CAVIARE AT THE FUNERAL

This was the village where the deacon
ate all the caviare at the funeral.
> Chekhov, "In the Ravine"

On the way back from the cemetery
they discussed the funeral arrangements
and the sermon, "such a comfort to the family."

They crowded into the parlor.
It was hot, and voices were beginning to rise.
The deacon found himself beside a plate
heaped with caviare. He helped himself
to a spoonful. Then another.

Suddenly he became aware
that everyone's eyes were upon him,
ruin staring him in the face.
He turned pale. Then tried to carry it off—
one may as well be hanged for a sheep
as a lamb, et cetera.

Meeting their eyes with a stern expression
he took another spoonful,
and another. He finished the plate.

Next morning he was seen at the station
buying a ticket for Kurovskoye,
a village much like ours, only smaller.

CHOCOLATES

Once some people were visiting Chekhov.
While they made remarks about his genius
the Master fidgeted. Finally
he said, "Do you like chocolates?"

They were astonished, and silent.
He repeated the question,
whereupon one lady plucked up her courage
and murmured shyly, "Yes."

"Tell me," he said, leaning forward,
light glinting from his spectacles,
"what kind? The light, sweet chocolate
or the dark, bitter kind?"

The conversation became general.
They spoke of cherry centers,
of almonds and Brazil nuts.
Losing their inhibitions
they interrupted one another.
For people may not know what they think
about politics in the Balkans,
or the vexed question of men and women,

but everyone has a definite opinion
about the flavor of shredded coconut.
Finally someone spoke of chocolates filled with liqueur,
and everyone, even the author of *Uncle Vanya,*
was at a loss for words.

As they were leaving he stood by the door
and took their hands.
                    In the coach returning to Petersburg
they agreed that it had been a most
unusual conversation.

THE MAN SHE LOVED

In the dusk
men with sidelocks, wearing hats
and long black coats walked side by side,
hands clasped behind their backs,
talking Yiddish. It was like being in a foreign country.

The members of the family
arrived one by one . . .
his aunts, his uncle, and his mother
talking about her business
in Venezuela. She had moved to a new building
with enough space and an excellent location.

To their simple, affectionate questions
he returned simple answers.
For how could he explain what it meant to be a writer . . .
a world that was entirely different,
and yet it would include the sofa
and the smell of chicken cooking.

Little did they know as they spoke
that one day they would be immortal
in a novel that commanded the sweep
of Tolstoy, a magnificent creation
that would bring within its compass
offices in Manhattan and jungles
of the Amazon. A grasp of psychology
and sense of the passing of time
that can only be compared to,
without exaggerating, Proust.

The path wound through undergrowth.
Palms rose at an angle from the humid plain.
He passed a hut with chickens and goats . . .
an old man who sat with his back to a wall,
not seeing. A woman came out of a door
and stared after him.
                              In the distance
the purple mountains shone, fading
as the heat increased.

"Let me take a look at it,"
said Joey. He took the watch
from Beth, pried open the back,
and laid it on the table before him.
He reached in his jacket
and produced a jeweler's loupe . . .
screwed it into his eye,
and examined the works.
"I can fix it. It only needs an adjustment."

"Are you sure?" said his sister.
"I wouldn't want anything to happen to it.
Jack gave it to me."

The used-car tycoon. But they never married.
"I've got," he said, "a tiger by the tail,"
meaning the used-car business.

Joey stared at her.
"Don't you think I know my business?"

Siblings. Members of the one family,
tied by affection, and doubt . . .
right down to the funeral
when, looking at the face in the box,
you can be sure. "That's real enough."

Spreading her wings at the piano . . .
"The Man I Love." A pleasant voice
but thin.

She traveled to Central America
on the Grace Line, singing with a band.
White boats on a deep blue sea . . .
at night a trail of fireflies.
"Sitting at the Captain's table,"
"Teeing off at the Liguanea Club."

This picture was taken much earlier . . .
three flappers with knee-high skirts.
1921.
They were still living in Delancey Street.

The songs that year were "Say It With Music"
and "If You Would Care For Me."

IV

PETER

1

At the end of the lane a van moving slowly . . .
a single tree like a palm rising above the rest . . .
so this is all there is to it,
your long-sought happiness.

2

On winter nights when the moon
hung still behind some scaffolding
you thought, "Like a bird in a cage."
You were always making comparisons . . .
"finding similitudes in dissimilars,"
says Aristotle. A form of insanity . . .
Nothing is ever what it appears to be,
but always like something else.

3

One has been flung down with its roots in the air.
Another tilts at an angle.
One has lost a limb in the storm
and stands with a white wound.
And one, covered with vines,
every May puts out a mass of flowers.

4

Poetry, says Baudelaire, is melancholy:
the more we desire, the more we shall have to grieve.
Devour a corpse with your eyes; art consists
in the cultivation of pain.
Stupidity reassures you; you do not belong
in a bourgeois establishment, it can never be your home.
Restlessness is a sign of intelligence;
revulsion, the flight of a soul.

MARIA ROBERTS

In the kingdom of heaven
there is neither past nor future,
but thinking, which is always present.

So it is, at this moment
I am sitting with Maria Roberts
and her young brother, Charles,
in a tram in the South Camp Road.

We are going to the Carib Theater.
But first we shall have to wait
for the tram coming in the other direction.
It seems that we shall spend eternity

staring at the nearest roofs,
trees with the bark shelling off—
eucalyptus—
a hedge that is powdered with dust.

Specks in the sky slowly circling . . .
crows. They seem to hang there.
Like Charley . . . he was shot down
over Germany during the war.

But Maria . . . in the Uffizi
the slender golden Venus,
gray eyes that gaze back at me . . .
must be living still somewhere.

The tram comes around the corner
finally, clanging its gong,
and passes . . . rows of dresses
and trousers and straw hats.

In the last row, the old women
with clay pipes stuck in their teeth
and baskets packed with vegetables
at their feet . . . Going to market.

Then our motorman climbs down
and throws the switch with his pole,
and we're off again, to the theater.
Today they're playing "The Firefly."

In the kingdom of heaven
there is neither past nor future,
but thinking, which is always present:

specks in the sky slowly circling,
a hedge that is covered with dust.

ARMIDALE

For George d'Almeida

Il faut voyager loin
en aimant sa maison.

AS A MAN WALKS

It's a strange country,
strange for me to have come to.
Cattle standing in a field,
sheep that are motionless
as stones,
the sun sinking in a pile of clouds,
and the eternal flies
getting in your ears and eyes . . .

I suppose you become accustomed.
Mrs. Scully was in her kitchen
entertaining two friends
when one said, "Isn't that a snake?"
and pointed. Sure enough
one was sliding around the divider.
She reached for something, the rolling pin,
and stunned it. Then finished it off
with a hammer.

The green-hide and stringy-bark Australian . . .
my candidate for survival
in the event of fire, flood,
or nuclear explosion.

As a man walks he creates the road he walks on.
All of my life in America
I must have been reeling out of myself
this red dirt, gravel road.

Three boys seated on motorcycles
conferring . . .

                        A little further on,
a beaten-up Holden parked off the road
with two men inside passing the bottle.
Dark-skinned . . . maybe they are aboriginal.

I might have been content to live
in Belle Terre, among houses and lawns,
but inside me are gum trees,
and magpies, cackling and whistling,
and a bush-roaming kangaroo.

A NUCLEAR FAMILY

The closest I ever came was the zoo.
There was the whole mob lying down
at one end of the compound. And one
really big one, the Old Man,
lying on his side, on his elbow
it looked like. With big hind legs
and tail, and funny drooping forepaws
held high in fly-swatting position.
He seemed asleep, but that was only
the look they all have, sleeping or waking,
the eye concealed by the orb
of the big lid curving down . . .
a look of shyness
or some sweet meditation.

But he's not like that, he's a tough one,
Old Man Kangaroo.
I can see him, after the day's work,
standing in the pub with his mates
talking against the Company.
Then, later, reeling home.
As a man walks he creates the road,
the moon gliding above the housetops
and the shadows.

When he comes in, there's his Missus
in the kitchen, lip curled in scorn.
He decides to brazen it out
(a veteran he of many night sorties) . . .
"Let's ha'e a bit o' dinner, then.
I'm about clammed."

She flares up. "Wheer's my money?
Wheer do I come in?
You've had a good jaunt,
tea waiting and washed up,
then you come crawling in.
You suppose, do you, I'm going to keep house for you
while you make a holiday?
You must think something of yourself."

"Don't be gettin thysen in a roar,"
he says, retreating at once, like a veteran.
He pulls a knotted kerchief out of his moleskin
and unties it with miner's fingers,
clumsy from the pick-work.

"Here's thy blessed money,
thy shillings an thy sixpences,"
pouring it on the table.
Then he reaches a hand to her shoulder,
"Now gie us summat, gie us a kiss."

"Behave thysen," she says, pushing him away,
"the child'll see."

"What child?" He looks around. "What?
Is the dear everywhere? I don't see him.
Are his eyes in the wall?"

"Enow o' thy clatter.
I never seen a rip as th'art.
Shall y'ave your dinner warmed?"

"Ay," he says, "an wi' a smite o' cheese."

A BUSH BAND

A guitar and drum,
a pole with bottlecaps nailed to it . . .

struck with a piece of wood
it gives off a silvery, joyful sound.

The woman playing the guitar
is sinewy, like the men in the ballad.

Driving their cattle overland
from Broome to Glen Garrick . . .

Cows low, wagon wheels turn,
red dust hangs in the air.

Some give their lives to cattle
and some to the words of a song,

arriving together at Glen Garrick
and at the end of the song.

DEATH OF THUNDERBOLT

Here he came to a place where two creeks meet,
a gouge in the earth, dry rocks . . .
yet when it rains it can drown you.

Barren and desolate, unless you're an aborigine
when every rock hides the spirit
of one of your departed relatives.

And for those who know the story
there is the figure of Constable Walker
in the saddle, looking down
at Fred Ward, known as Thunderbolt.

Ward is halfway across the creek
on foot, having released his horse
so as to double back to it later.
An old trick of the bushranger . . .
but the constable isn't having any,
he's caught up with Thunderbolt at last.

While parrots flutter in a tree
and a kookaburra laughs like a maniac,
Ward speaks. "Are you a policeman?"
"I am," says Walker. "You surrender."
Then Ward says, "Have you a family?"
to which the constable answers,
"I thought of that before I came here."
And he says again, "You surrender."
"I'll die first," says Ward.

Then the constable, raising his revolver
and shouting "You and I for it!"
struck spur to his horse.

But the beast missed its footing
almost throwing him down.
Ward ran forward and grabbed him by the arm . . .
the constable pressed the muzzle of the revolver
against Ward's body, and fired.
Ward attempted to grasp him again . . .
the constable struck him over the head
with the butt of the revolver. And Ward fell.

Walker stood, to recover his breath,
then lifted Ward under the arms
and half carried, half dragged him onto the bank.
The bushranger's eyes were closed
and there was a stain on his shirt
where the bullet had gone in.

Scarcely believing what had happened,
it all happened so fast,
his own actions appearing like a dream,
the constable mounted and rode back to Uralla.

Where the Coachwood and Cedar Motor Hotel
now stands, at the head of a street
full of shops and offices where men sit
counting money.

But at dusk when the lights shine on
in the little streets and the surrounding hills,
what would the children do without a story?

Getting to his feet, walking back
to his horse that whinnies in a shadow . . .
He climbs in the saddle and rides
into the bush where he still lives.

ARMIDALE

The window propped with a nail, gazing across a valley, tawny, with occasional trees, dark green exotics and a crown of gum trees, olive-green or gray against the tawny, lion-skinned earth . . .

The gum trees are "dying back." Some woods appear to have been shelled—there are only white trunks and naked branches. No one seems to know the reason. Some say it's the Christmas beetle—where trees are sparse the beetles concentrate on the trees that are left and consume the foliage. So that more trees die.

The morning air is fresh, the sky light blue without a cloud. We are in the middle of April—Autumn at the antipodes. Where have I felt this quality of the atmosphere, this coolness together with an unclouded sky? In the South of France thirty years ago. The landscape, however, was different, with terraces and rows of vines. The veranda gazed on a sparkling blue sea, the shallows streaked with red. There were flowers, a garden full of flowers. And poppies along the road.

The years between are wiped out by memory. Once again the novelist of the "madeleine" comes to mind: a taste or sensation repeated after an interval of years will return you to the first time you had it, so that the years disappear. Memory walks onto the stage and lifts the hills and carries them away. One is left with the naked stage.

The coast of the South of France brings another in its train. I am in Jamaica, by the pool at Bournemouth, reading Proust for the first time. Wandering in the Guermantes Way I am oblivious to the swaying palms and the waves breaking along the shore. At sixteen I didn't give a damn for the nature that attended me everywhere, Wordsworth's tireless nurse, arching me over with her blue sky in which a mass of white clouds were heaped, fresh from the laundry. I would much rather have had Gloria to look at or Peter to talk to.

I don't know that I've changed: I still want human company. But now I look at nature with a thoughtful eye. The sheer persistence of her behavior strikes me as having some significance behind it. Why do the fields keep returning in their colors, tawny or green? These shining skies . . . it's as though they were saying, Look at us! Consider the light on sea and land. It is what remains.

But people walk around on the surface of the earth, under the sky, without taking notice of it. Not once do they consider the earth and the wonders thereof. They don't give a hoot about nature.

I suppose this is understandable. Nature isn't a kindly nurse. In Australia when you walk into the scene that looked fine at a distance, you are attacked by flies. They get into your ears and eyes. The fields are dry, the foliage monotonous —it takes a practised eye to find variety in gum trees. Yet this is good cattle and sheep grazing country. Think what it is like in the interior! The middle of Australia is a great emptiness.

This may account for the pessimism of the Australian and his tendency to "knock"—the deeper in, the worse it gets. In America from the beginning when people were dissatisfied they were able to move to a better place. But there is no better place in Australia—the first was best, around the edge, where colonies were planted. Outback is desert and rocks. The Australian psyche answers to this geography. People don't want to venture inland—they don't want to explore the Unconscious, they know it will be a desert. They cling to the coastal rim and towns. They stand elbow to elbow in the public bar and stupefy their senses with beer. They are satisfied with betting on horses or watching football on TV.

There once was a race that knew how to live in the interior. The aborigine walked from one watering place to another. He knew a tree that gushed water when you tapped it, and where springs ran underground. He would walk to a place where herbs were coming into harvest, and stay there a while, then walk to another place. He knew how to set fire to the trunks of trees so that plants would grow. This was an exact science: the fire could be set only in the one month out of twelve—at any other time, firing trees would wipe out the crop.

The Outback was not a wilderness to the aborigine— the spirits of his ancestors were there. They had to be propitiated and consulted. From puberty until middle age the male aborigine was engaged in rites of passage: he walked about like a scholar at the University of Gottingen, with extreme caution and the sense of a very thick, multilayered culture. If anything, the lives of these people were too steeped in culture. A mistake could have fatal consequences: the aborigine who, without being licensed to do so, discovered the hiding-places of the tablets of the tribe, and looked upon and handled them, could expect to be put to death.

The white man saw all this walking about as shiftlessness. He fenced the aborigine off from his burying grounds and broke his connection with the spirits. He prevented him from getting at the food he liked, and when the aborigine stole a sheep, the white man branded him a criminal, put him in chains, and shipped him to a prison where he died. He chopped him up and fed his flesh to the dogs. Then the white man was left with a great emptiness to confront, the Australian desert.

But he doesn't confront it. He puts his head down and mends his fences. He argues about the Union—shorter hours and better pay. The rest of his time is given to distractions.

I am not accusing the Australian—he is the white man everywhere, flourishing on the outside and empty within. This continent is like a projection of our inner state. We are all clinging to the edge and asking for distractions. Australia is like a screen on which we see the deserts of the psyche in an age of mass-production.

Far from criticizing the Australian, we may admire those who, in this harsh environment, have had significant lives. Daisy Bates, for example . . . in her leg-o'-mutton sleeves and long Victorian skirt and veil of mosquito netting. Daisy lived among the aborigines and was privy to their secrets. She shared her food with them and nursed them when they were sick. Daisy was a secular saint; very few people could live as she did, with no separation between "real life" and the life of the mind.

This is not what the future appears to hold for the rest of us. In his novel *Voss,* Patrick White suggests what may actually happen. The hero and heroine, being far apart from each other, and increasingly removed from pleasure in their own physical existence—he is exploring the wilderness and she is living among middle-class people in Melbourne—construct images of each other in their heads. As their lives become less physical, these images appear more real.

If we cannot live with nature as they used to in Devon, then the answer may be to do without nature and construct images and address ourselves to them. It is the hermetic idea: after all we are what we think we are—our bodies are not very permanent. The answer may be to live in a fantasy.

I am not looking forward to it. I don't want to live "against nature" like a Symbolist or a Surrealist. But as bureaucracy triumphs over every foot of the earth's surface, and men go to their labor like ants, and huddle in multi-level buildings above the ground or in tunnels beneath it, they may have to find their happiness in illusions. There will be generations that have never touched a leaf. Millions of people in the United States are already living this way.

But whereas the Symbolists and Surrealists created their illusions, in the future illusions will be provided. The masses will sit gazing at pictures of green hills and breaking waves, with the appropriate sounds. They won't even have to applaud—they will hear the sound of applause. Access to the real thing will be prohibited to all but a few thousand members of the ruling political party.

The alternative is for our space-explorers to come upon a habitable planet, some place of green earth and clear water, within navigable distance.

OUT OF SEASON

Once I stayed at the Grand Hotel
at Beaulieu, on the Mediterranean.
This was in May. A wind blew steadily
from sea to land, banging the shutters.
Now and then a tile would go sailing.

At lunch and dinner we ate fish soup
with big, heavy spoons.
Then there would be fish, then the main course.

At the next table sat an old woman
and her companion, Miss O'Shaughnessy
who was always writing letters
on the desk in the lounge provided for that purpose—
along with copies of *Punch* and *The Tatler*
and an old wind-up Victrola.

There was a businessman from Sweden
and his secretary. She had a stunning figure
on the rocks down by the sea.
She told me, "My name is Helga.
From Vasteras" . . . brushing her hair,
leaning to the right, then to the left.

Also, an Englishman who looked ill
and went for walks by himself.

———

I remember a hotel in Kingston
where our mother used to stay
when she came on one of her visits
from America. It was called
the Manor House. There was a long veranda
outside our rooms, and peacocks on the lawn.

We played badminton and golf,
and went swimming at Myrtle Bank.
I did jigsaw puzzles, and water colors,
and read the books she had brought.

In the lounge there were newspapers
from America . . . "Gas House Gang Conquer Giants."
What I liked were the cartoons,
"The Katzenjammer Kids" and "Bringing Up Father."

———

Getting back to Beaulieu . . .
this could have been one of the places
where the Fitzgeralds used to stay—
the bedroom thirty feet across,
a ceiling twelve feet high.
The bathroom, also, was enormous.

A voice would say . . . "Avalon,"
followed by the sound of an orchestra,
and . . . shuffling. This would continue
all night, till two or three,
when the last pair of feet went away.

I was preparing to shave
when an arm came out of the wall.
It was holding a tennis racket.
It waved it twice, moved sideways,
flew up, and vanished through the ceiling.

———

Of course not. Yet, it's weird
how I remember the banging shutters
and the walk to the village
past cork trees and slopes lined with vines.

Narrow, cobbled streets going down to the sea . . .
There would be boats drawn up, and nets
that a fisherman was always mending.

I sat at a table overlooking the Mediterranean.
At the next table sat the Englishman
who looked unwell. I nodded.

He paid for his drink abruptly
and strode away. Terrified
that I might want his company.

———

At times like this, when I am away from home
or removed in some other way,
it is as though there were another self
that is waiting to find me alone.

Whereupon he steps forward:
"Here we are again, you and me . . .
and sounds . . . the chirping of birds
and whispering of leaves,
the sound of tires passing on the road."

Yes, and images . . . Miss O'Shaughnessy
shouting "Fish soup!" in the old woman's ear.
The businessman from Vasteras
and his girl . . . lying on her side,
the curve of her body
from head to slender feet.

The Englishman walking ahead of me . . .
He has a stick; as he walks
he slashes with it at the reeds
that are growing beside the road.

These things make an unforgettable impression,
as though there were a reason for being here,
in one place rather than another.

THE MEXICAN WOMAN

All he needed was fifty cents
to get to a job in Union City.

You wouldn't believe it, he
was in Mexico with Black Jack Pershing.

He lived with a Mexican woman.
Then he followed her, and was wise.

"Baby," he said, "you're a two-timer,
I'm wise to you and the lieutenant."

———

I gave him the fifty cents,
but the old man's tale still haunts me.

I know what it's like to serve
in Mexico with Black Jack Pershing.

And to walk in the dust and heat . . .
for I can see her hurrying

to the clay wall where they meet,
and I shall be wise to her and the lieutenant.

AN IRISH POET

Three blue dragonflies have settled
on my net. I'm through for the day.
I put down the rod, ship oars,
and lie, reading as I drift
the *Collected Poems* of Patrick Kavanagh.

I met Kavanagh once, in New York
at a party. Some literary agent
had brought along her young daughter . . .
sixteen or seventeen, with a bare midriff
and a very short skirt.

Kavanagh went over and talked to her.
She laughed once or twice
then made as though to move away.
Whereupon he raked his fingernails
down her back. They were black with dirt.

Later he went around asking everyone
"Have you seen my Baby Doll?"

———

How relieved Kavanagh must have been
to get back to Dublin!
Away from all the clever New Yorkers,
so well informed about politics
and literature and art . . .

back to his personal quarrels.
I can see him coming along the canal
at the Holy Hour, the pubs having closed,
rehearsing what he ought to have said
to the man in Grogan's, the goat-faced penny-a-liner.

He sits on a bench by the canal
gazing up into a tree
that whispers like the boughs of the heart.
A sky with soft, pearly clouds
such as you get in Ireland . . .

Where the clouds are torn the sun
blazing, the air electric blue.

BACK IN THE STATES

It was cold, and all they gave him to wear
was a shirt. And he had malaria.

There was continual singing of hymns—
"Nearer My God to Thee" was a favorite.
And a sound like running water . . .
it took him a while to figure it.

Weeping, coming from the cells
of the men who had been condemned.

Now here he was, back in the States,
idly picking up a magazine,
glancing through the table of contents.

Already becoming like the rest of us.

ABOUT THE AUTHOR

Louis Simpson has had a long and distinguished career in American letters. He is the author of eight volumes of poetry, among them *At the End of the Open Road, Adventures of the Letter I,* and, most recently, *Searching for the Ox.* Among his important critical studies are *A Revolution in Taste* and *Three on the Tower.* An autobiography, *North of Jamaica,* and a novel, *Riverside Drive,* depict his life in the West Indies and on New York's West Side. He has received many honors and awards, among them the Prix de Rome, *The Hudson Review* Fellowship, the Columbia University Medal for Excellence, two Guggenheim Fellowships, and the Pulitzer Prize for Poetry. Louis Simpson has been Professor of English and Comparative Literature at the State University of New York at Stony Brook since 1967.

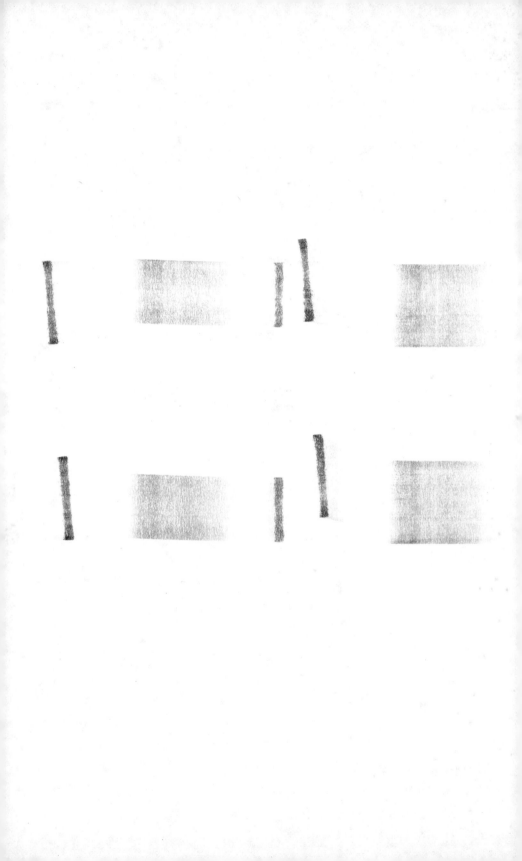